reminded of something

Robin Thomas

Cinnamon Press
:: small miracles from distinctive voices ::

Published by Cinnamon Press
www.cinnamonpress.com

ISBN 978-1-78864-144-9

British Library Cataloguing in Publication Data. A CIP record for this book can be obtained from the British Library.

Designed and typeset in Bodoni by Cinnamon Press. Cover design by Adam Craig © Adam Craig.

Cinnamon Press is represented by Inpress

Robin Thomas completed the MA in Writing Poetry at Kingston University in 2012. He has had poems published in the following journals: *Acumen, Agenda, Envoi, Orbis, Brittle Star, Poetry Salzburg, Poetry Scotland, Pennine Platform, The High Window, South, Stand, Rialto* and *The Interpreter's House*. He has been shortlisted for the Buzzwords, Bridport and Bath Poetry Café prizes and is represented in several anthologies. His pamphlet, *A Fury of Yellow*, was published by Eyewear in November, 2016. His debut collection, *Momentary Turmoil*, was published in 2018, followed by *A Distant Hum* in 2021, both with Cinnamon Press. Dempsey and Windle published his *Cafferty* pamphlet in 2021 and his collection, *Weather on the Moon*, was published by Two Rivers Press in 2022. Robin also had a flash fiction novella, *Margot and the Strange Objects*, published by Adhoc Publishing in 2022.

Acknowledgements

Thanks to my many friends on the poetry scenes in Reading, Bath, London and elsewhere and to Todd Swift, Jan Fortune, Adam Craig, Janice Dempsey, Peter Robinson and Anne Nolan for their support and advice.

Thanks are also due to the editors of the following, in which some of these poems previously appeared: *Acumen, Agenda, Envoi, Orbis, Brittle Star, Pennine Platform, The High Window, Poetry Scotland, South, Poetry Salzburg Review, Stand, Rialto, The Interpreters House* and *North*.

Contents

III

IV

For my wife Mary, who died in October 2021

reminded of something

The Engine

Who remembers the birches
which swayed in the soft winds
of yesterday? And who recalls
the fires of their heart

when the sky was blue and the sun
a hot engine, driving through winter
to spring, through spring towards
joy; or the child which played

at the foot of the birch trees
which swayed in the bickering wind,
drifting tomorrow
onto its innocent head?

I

After many a season

all the things she was
compressed
expanded
to become
an event
and curtains closing

I
was just getting to know her

Window

I thought we were on the same train: she
looking out of the window at the world streaking by,
me sitting next to her, reading,
then getting up to stretch my legs,
while our world roared,
swayed, jerked, clattered.

And so we were, but what I didn't see was
that our trains were also diverging,
that while I wandered the aisles, talking to friends,
sharing jokes, she could see, through the window,
our lives flashing by, and something
she hadn't seen before,

something that looked at her, as if it
might hold sway over her,
something that drew this other train away,
towards somewhere I wasn't going
yet. When I sat down again,
I saw your face was pale.

The country station

The train stopped at one of those country stations
with benches and tubs of flowers on the platform
and not much else. There was a stream nearby
that you could see from it, or maybe a river
almost out of sight. There was white fencing,
a horse in a field, a cow, or sheep. The sun shone
or rain pelted down like a handful of gravel
thrown at a window. A road led somewhere, perhaps.

She got off, saying she needed to do something
but would follow me by the next train. Ours
began to move and I leaned out of the window.
We smiled at each other and as the train gathered speed
she got smaller and smaller, both of us making
'see you soon' signals until she was a tiny dot
still not walking away as the train rounded a bend
and only trees could be seen.

On listening to a Brahms piano concerto

How you would have loved it:
the power, the expression,
the tenderness ... h'mm, let's try again:
the thunder, the sweetness of rain,
mild, fresh mornings, impenetrable
night ... well, anyway: its shape,
the compulsiveness of it, its
unstoppability.

If there's a somewhere
you've gone,
I doubt
there'll be anything like it.

The house is silent

unless I turn the radio on, or whistle
or talk to myself, or the floorboards creak
or sound comes in from outside: wind perhaps,
chainsaws or delivery vans.

She's left her books, her clothes, her piano,
drawings, sketchbooks, paints, her herbal teas,
the wardrobe she got from an auction, her table,
cushions, the bench her father made,
vases, magazines, bicycle, car, keys,
money, passport, papers, reminders
on Post-it Notes (don't sit too long, try
not to slump) her mother's paintings, address books,
wrapping paper, shopping lists, and me.

Where won't you next be

1. You don't

pull back the curtains
to look at the sky,
switch on the news,
bring the radio down,

go into the kitchen,
open the fridge,
have a look at your sketchbook
while stirring the eggs,

put in the washing,
step into the garden
to bring back some herbs,
help me make our bed.

2. There's no

welcome home
when I come through the door.
As I lock it behind me I don't
keep you safe.

Something, nothing

What was supposed to happen
was nothing: fear, sleepless nights,
but in the end, nothing, and relief.

But something did happen,
something we had no expectation of,
being immortal,

immortal,
because not to be so
is intolerable.

So, it happened:
worry, then fear, then terror,
then nothing.

Dad, pictured

I wish you weren't in that picture
crafted by Mary in 1989. You,
and no-one else,
are who I need now.
Come and sit here.
You don't need to say anything.
Please, just come.
But you won't, will you.
You have to stay there.

Hobby

I

After breakfast he would
go and work on his models—
preparing, measuring, cutting,
assembling—then he would
polish them to completion.
A final look, and, as soon as
the opportunity arose, he would
give them away, which is
how you got here.

II

I remember him making me.
I felt his love for me growing
as I took shape, felt it
more and more as I became
what I am. Slide my drawers out,
what do you feel? Each one
contains something of him
and look, in the bottom one,
something that feels like a brooch.

Mrs Jones, the dads and me

Mrs Jones prepares to cross the road
with her baby, children and dog,
one hand on the pram and the dog's lead,
the other shared by two

> I see her from the passenger seat
> of the car my dad drives, the seat
> I'm standing on. Oh, the joy
> of it, I won't sit down.

leaping, jumping children. She must
control all this, look both ways and cross.
Although this is impossible,
she, with a little help, succeeds

> No, I won't. The world is mine.
> When I stand on the bouncing seat,
> I can see what grown-ups see,
> but not the future, because my dad

with ease and fun. Oh, how she loves
her children and her life and life.
The dads are spellbound
and stop for her, giving her safe passage.

> like the other dads, sees a woman,
> and a pram, children, dog
> and because my dad is kind, he stops,
> presses the brake just

And on she goes

    too heavily

along the street

    and I

  Bash!

Room 49

My mother is in a womb,
all needs supplied,
and I, who came from hers,
can enter and hold her hand.
If I talk, she doesn't respond:
she doesn't have language,
or if she has, it's not one I speak.

She floats in warmth.
A song comes
from somewhere distant.
She is sloughing off her self.
She is preparing
for birth into the universe.

The day my mother died

was as perfect as you could imagine:
a deep blue sky, Spring, shadows, light
in every shade from every direction—
brick red, mauve, white—a handful
of birch trees, a table and umbrella,
a door wide open, a small breeze,
a breath of leaves on the parasol—
transparent colour and movement—
wisteria bunching, hanging
and shifting, an alertness of jay,
a self-containment of bees, silver greens,
yellow greens, light, dark, orange-flecked,
a straightness of bricks, a brevity of blossom,
sage, thyme and marjoram.

I went through the door to make some tea.
I took out a teaspoon and closed the drawer,
closed it clumsily trapping my finger.

The photos

Shot after shot of Weymouth, Chichester, Poole,
castles, sea, flowers, strangers,
black and white buildings, shopping malls, plants,
parks, ponds, nieces, cousins, grandchildren, us,
best friend Norma, all in albums:
'Ireland', 'Swanage', 'More eightieth birthday'
'Keith's new house' (no photos yet),
all labelled as if for an exam or project.
I tease them from the sleeves they
don't want to leave; I save some
for her to never see, throw the rest,
take the empty albums to Oxfam.

I could have kept them all,
put them on a shelf somewhere,
or in the loft. Why not? But why?

The Red Ball

I

I see
a ball
into being.
I see it,
feel it,
squeeze it,
devour
its redness.

II

Gordon Barker, having defended
and blocked, blocked and defended,
now lofts a cover drive, one bounce,
over the rope and thump! into my memory.

I feel
the ball's seam
in my fingers.
I toss it up
to Gordon Barker.

Will he block?
Will he nurdle?
Will he middle it?
I haven't decided.

Ardnamurchan Point

In summer, when we encountered
that uncommon event—a day that smiled—
we would pack ourselves into our old car
with sandwiches and flasks
and set out for Ardnamurchan Point.

The way there of course is not straight,
nor is it level, but there is much to see,
much to marvel at, although our keenness
to reach our destination would cause us
to see less than we might have.

At last we would near it, see its name
on signposts, though there was little indication
of how far it was. Still we would drive on,
as the day grew tired and the road
which would take us there more twisted.

More twisted, and yet more twisted,
so that sometimes the road seemed to
go back on itself; narrower
and bumpier too, as the day, which had started
friendly, now took on a solemn aspect.

Surely we would see it
over the brow of the next hill, or
the one after that? But the day
would mouth 'Stop' and we would turn back.
We would never reach Ardnamurchan Point.

Origins

They waddle, squabbling, round me,
those on the bank. One
comes right up to me and stares.
I drop it a pellet which bounces off its beak.
It doesn't even look for it but peers,
unwavering, into my face.

I have 'swan and duck food'
from a hardware shop.
I cast most of it into the river
where the birds scrabble for it,
snap each pellet down
as if it were life itself.

But the river—from where the floating birds
can see the flying food, see it floating near them,
can each get some because there's plenty—
isn't good enough for my goose, whose eyes say:
let them splash and fight and screech,
that's not for me. It steps now
actually onto my sandalled foot:

Oi!, I'm first!; or, *you don't look edible to me;*
or, *make me your best friend, dog-like*
but with feathers; or, *which button should I push?*
or, *I beseech thee, Oh Supreme Being, drop thou*
a pellet to thine acolyte and I shall be thine forever;
or, *I'm standing on your foot, you wally. Give them to me!*

Their own lives

After Larkin, 'Afternoons'

Something is pushing them
To the side of their own lives

That something is Nature
which pays no heed to
swings and sandpits,
albums, televisions,
acorn collecting, laundry; but
is very keen on courting,
husbands, trades (skilled
or otherwise), and especially
it cares about beauty,
until it's done its job.

Grandmothers

It wasn't in battle, his ship blasted from under him,
or keeling over as the sea poured in,
or a trawlerman's defeat by vicious waves;
nor did he swim out too far in swirling currents.

No. Just a day out, with sandwiches
and flasks of tea, him fishing nearby
in the friendly river, which turned on him,
swept him away as he slid on the familiar mud.

And now, must *I* face it?
My first sight of it since…
She swims for the school.
She loves it, trusts it. My choice?

Avoid the hated element, or
be that grandmother, doting, as we should.
And I can do it: it's contained in slab sides,
her swimming is strong, there are

life-guards, other swimmers, watchers
who would dive in, their clothes wrapped
to their bodies. I will face it down, be that loving person,
will smile and clap, as grandmothers do.

Pickled walnuts, bags of salt

Between 'Chilled Fish and Seafood'
and 'Cooked Meats, Deli & Dips',
a sabre tooth tiger, its back
level with the cabinet tops,
its shoulders wide as the aisle,
its fangs in a deadly curve,
its eyes for killing.

The shoppers clatter their trolleys
up and down the aisles, slow down, signal,
push them together, build barriers of them,
collect tins—of peas, of lentils
in tomato sauce, boneless
sardines—jars of olives stuffed with pimento,
pickled walnuts, bags of salt,
divide themselves in groups,
surround the beast,
and in a frenzy of roaring, screaming, thrashing,
and in a hail of missiles, slaughter it.

The science of poetry

It was not, he said, until forty-five years after publication that Keats's error—it had not been 'stout Cortez' on that mountain—was noticed. But Richardson was wrong: Tennyson had mentioned it to Palgrave who had put a footnote in the *Treasury.* Even that was not the earliest: it was spotted, by an unknown worker in the field, as early as 1845. Generously maintaining his anonymity he suggested that it be corrected should there be any future editions of the poet's work.

Angie's Song

after Yeats, 'The Song of Wandering Aengus'

I crouched to peer at a fallen leaf
and we were the only things in the world.
You gave me a box of stickies,
and I was happy as a balloon. I jumped
over a toadstool to become a Brownie
—oh, what a day—the best day of my life,
I skipped

        into a long tube. Blinking,
I walked out of the other end
with my ticket. It was smudged, or
out of focus. An escalator
towered above me. I should step on,
everyone said. So, looking up, I
grasped the handrail.

Life and work

The stones of Vienna
are not embedded in the structure of the Waldstein.
The first bars of the Pastoral are not composed
of Prince Lichnowsky's golden florins. 'No!',
said Amalie, Josephine, Antonie, Therese—
but this is not the repetition
at the Diabelli's heart. And Karl's near death
does not unproblematically inform
the *Adagio molto espressivo* of opus 127.

But his unprepared-for journey to Vienna
in an open cart in 'twenty seven
following that year's events
did nothing to prolong his life:
no more Beethoven, no more music.
That much can be said.

At home

Vanessa Bell, 'The Other Room', 1939

One stares
through the french windows.
Another sits, head in hands.
A third dozes on a sofa.

(Madrid. South Wales.
Love. Famine. Hate.
Czechoslovakia. Lies.
Displacement. Nanjing.
Kindness. Non-Aggression Pact.
Hope. Fear. Disappointment.)

Sofa, curtains and chairs
glow with careful life.
Flowers are suitably arranged
in orange and white.

They
have no idea what to do.

The artist and the woman

Guercino, 'The woman taken in adultery', c.1621

The man on the right,
whose hair is grey and beard long,
who stands so easily tall and straight,
must surely be defending that woman.

The two young men
incline their heads, perhaps
towards a change of mind.
'Who's right?' they seem to say, 'We
are simple men but ready
to weigh arguments, eschew
the leap to judgement.'

That intelligent-looking man,
head angled to persuade,
his expression suggestive of
charity, understanding, logic,
is not needed surely?

Sonnet 12 for the 21st century

I have a space-time clock.
Wherever I go it tells me the time.
Whatever the time it knows where I am.
So if I fly off, as I sometimes do,
into our galaxy, or more rarely, the next,
I can always find out where-when I am,
useful when I want to come back,
the way being difficult, the directions vague.

One day I shall want to return, and
will rummage around for my clock
and find it, and shake it, and bash it and panic
and realise
that time-space's scythe
had done what it does.

Mrs Jesson's brush with life

After David Lean, 'Brief Encounter', 1945

'Don't forget your glasses Laura!'

And so to Milford
for boiled fish,
a senseless film,
a toothbrush,
a hideous clock for Fred.

She hears the whistle. She
steps outside to see the train which ex-

plodes through the station,
screaming, smoking, showering
fragments of hot ash

and steps back inside where she finishes

that's an awfully nice-looking creature over there

her cup of tea.

The thing in the garden

She's studying a rock
which leans out over the sea
by the path which leads to Jenner
looking to extract its meaning.
She returns to her workshop
to fashion—a thing with a hole.
What was that meaning?
Nothing and nobody knows,
neither Hepworth, the rock,
nor the thing with a hole.

Aah, thank God, we can relax:
a thing with a hole
can be a thing with a hole.

Above it, above the thing,
and the marvellous, meaningless, garden,
the gulls sound out their furious non sense.

The utility room

After T.S.Eliot, 'Burnt Norton iv'

At the still point of the turning world
I fill the washing machine and switch
to *40 degrees + prewash*, listen to
the inrush of the waters, watch
my identities spin themselves
to cleanliness. Leaving,
I take a self to the kitchen,
brew—though it's already four o'clock—
breakfast tea. I am compelled
to watch the burial of the day.

All day I held the memory of you

after R.Brooke, 'One Day'

> *All the day*
> *I held the memory of you, and wove*
> *Its laughter with the dancing light o' the spray,*

Today my body has assembled
feelings of happiness and memories of you
out of stored data and sense impressions
in accordance with unyielding rules.
I can almost believe
this dancing light on the white waves
is real, and that you, you,
who seem to cause my heart to bound,
really do so, that you are not just
an instrument for our survival.

Late and soon

After Wordsworth

Let Triton blow his wreathèd horn
from ever deepening main to warn
of coming dangers: the world
is near beyond us, will unfurl
and yield, unless we stop and listen
to Her whose very heart we piss on.
'Use these, my sea and wind,' she begs,
'you're lounging on a powder keg.'

Gortnahoe

The wide blue sky, its nursery clouds,
the pebbledash bungalows,
the concrete church

which glows inside, vibrates
with music, incense, custom,
shafts of colour, desire, hope.

> Pilate condemns,
> he accepts the cross,
> he falls,
> his mother,
> Simon,
> Veronica,
> he falls again,
> is nailed up,
> dies.

'We all have doubts, especially
at this difficult time.
Why? We ask. *Why?*'

The bearers wilting, like he of Cyrene;
folk in the road, talking, subdued;
cars threading by, respectful.

A tall black vehicle, heading off,
the sun kindly,
the breeze soft.

Christmas Eve

A soft quiet hangs in the air
above a silveryness, and you
are tired, and we are tired
but content, after the wine and chatter.

We're walking home,
past decorated trees and nodding reindeer,
exchanging greetings as we go; above us
the lights of a plane coming in.

I point to it and cry, in mock amazement:
'Look, Father Christmas.'
'Father Christmas! Father Christmas!'
you shriek, and I am suddenly ashamed.

It's not far now. There will be
midnight mass in the church
at the end of the road. I'm wondering if
the vicar is feeling ashamed.

The specification

Here's a design for an ostrich's clavicle, here the muscle structure of a lizard's tail, here a colouring scheme for a zebra.

This is the visual cortex of a vole: sheet nine is on the board. The chief points to this connection, that, follows the circuits with his finger, asking, listening.

He goes back to his office, shutting the door, and can be seen, pondering. After a time he calls his best designers in, bids them sit, orders tea, asks them about their families.

I'm thinking of a new creature. Quite ordinary in many ways—you'll be able to adapt the designs you have for many of its features. Its brain will be quite complex, but we've done complex before.

But I'm looking as well for something entirely new—I want you to build into its circuitry what I'm going to call a 'moral framework', a set of commandments if you like.

And I want you to design it so the creature's free to break them and to decide whether to do so or not, oh, and make it its fault, if it does, not mine.

A beta version has been released

Teamwork

'Morning chaps. No, don't stand on ceremony—do be seated. Good. I've asked you to come here today to bring you up to date with events and to tell you how you fit in. Unroll the map Sergeant, please.

'Now *this* is where we're going—*here*—and the idea is that we smash Jerry from two sides, from *here*, and *here*. Your job is to make sure he can't escape, holding *this* position, *here*. You're to get off at first light tomorrow and get *here*, as fast as you can and when you do, you dig in. Now Jerry won't give in easily. That's where you come in. He'll come at you hard. There'll be quite a fight. But I know you Irish, you'll be itching to get your hands on 'em. So get yourselves some sleep, and see you tomorrow.'

'Entirely gratified Your Honour, but if we could only get our hands round that pretty neck of yours ...'

Lists

Included in Stalin's other list:
Shostakovich, Eisenstein,
who never knew
that there were two, and lived in terror.

Shostakovich carried on, needing only
pen, paper and piano. As did Eisenstein,
somehow procuring cameras,
film stock, lights, props, locations.

Symphonies 4, 5 and 6
Piano concertos 1 and 2
Lady Macbeth of Mtsensk
Alexander Nevsky
October
Ivan the Terrible

No one came to confiscate notebooks,
pencils or piano, or film-making equipment.
But one by one, actors, producers, assistants,
staff came in one day and not the next.

Anne spots a bird and is reminded of something

I hadn't been outside for so long that
everything in the natural world
seemed wonderful to me.
For a long time I hadn't even noticed it.
Then, for a moment, as I was being
loaded into a truck like a thing,
the world was full of
fluttering, chattering, swooping wonder.
But nothing lives here, even the living.

Houseproud

After Larkin, 'Home is so sad'

I didn't like their furniture,
especially that wardrobe,
hated their wallpaper
and the way they left stuff
everywhere. Why did they
play the piano when there was
tidying up to do? I didn't like
the noise their children made,
that visitors made—why
did they keep wine and beer?
Just to make more noise?

I'm here to protect humans
from wind and rain, and while
they sleep. So they need
to help me, by fixing the roof,
painting the windows,
clearing the gutters, not sit there
reading, or chatting or gossiping.
I want to be calm, neat and clean,
be well maintained and not
give offence to the house next door.

I was glad when they left,
taking their jumble of things,
that embarrassing wardrobe,
their rumbustious children.
Let's hope the next lot
will be more respectful.

Dark-eyed night

Invisible

On my street, after dark, outside the pub, where baleful yellow light spilled out, under whose doors leaked raucous noise, where the bus stop was with its filthy shelter, there was always a tribe of boys, the blood-curdling ugliness of their speech, their strident laughter and unearthly howls. They would push, argue, stamp out their cigarettes, fill the night with their exclusive being.

I would not go past for a million pounds, but sometimes I must, shrinking, invisible, or so I hoped.

[Lost souls blunder

Night

loneliness clatters through the tunnel

    queue for taxis   which do not arrive

here, is the entry: closed.

  a police car appears

     and disappears

doorway sleeper   doorway sleeper   doorway sleeper

        in front of mannequins, lonely as the yellow light

a fox tears rubbish from the bin bags

       under the lamps and shadows

laughter echoes   along the street   the girl looks,

and hurries away, her heels clicking in a fast beat

       through night's thick absence.

Ferry

I drive—
my only companion, my only comfort,

the soft-lit dials—
threading the dark

in an unknown country
of hills and water,

heading
for the bright-lit hotel I know is somewhere across the water.

At last, the ferry.
I have none of their money.

Here is only solitude,

The beating heart of the library

In the great library
on the towering shelves—
all the books ever written—
almanacs, bibles, histories, discoveries,
stories, philosophies, discourses, all
leading out, through their windows,
to worlds outside, inside worlds.
But none more truthful than the brief account
of an unending search on an amaranthine river,
for outside darkness,
the darkness inside.

and other solitudes,

When

When I had walked into that night
leaving behind me
all that belonged to the day.

When I had given up
all that was known and loved
and visible.

When you had been waiting in the day
for my return, and had made
all ready.

When you had realised that I
had been replaced by absence,
then your day too turned into night.

whose furious eyes

Confession

Here on the path between the church wall
and the graveyard, the gravel
asserting its ancientness, the mass of yew trees
its everlasting blackness, I make
my confession: I do not
believe in you, oh lord of all creation.

signal 'keep away'.

What can it be like

now you've ceased to be
now your eyes have closed
for the last time, and you
can't even see that it's dark?

Here are only tears,

The night sky is always

there, we hope

and pretence.]

The news

In the middle of an ordinary day, the
lunch things

still on the table, the news came,
and stood there.

I put the things away,
washed

what needed washing, carefully
hung

the dishcloth over the rail
and sat down.